Table of Contents

Introduction 1
Chapter 1: Let's Talk Travel Planning and Budgeting 5
Chapter 2: Picking Your Dream Spot and Wallet-Friendly Plans 8
Chapter 3: Finding Budget-Friendly Transportation .. 11
Chapter 4: Let's Talk Accommodations: Finding Your Home Away from Home 16
Chapter 5: Let's Plan Your Daily Adventures and Epic Experiences 20
Chapter 6: Navigating Food Costs on Your Travels .. 23
Chapter 7: Be Ready for Anything: Emergency Funds and Backup Plans 27
Chapter 8: Money Matters: Mastering Your Finances on the Fly 30
Chapter 9: Unveiling Travel Budget Hacks 33
Chapter 10: Learning from Your Adventure: Reflecting on Your Travel Experience and Budgeting Smarts 38

Introduction

Hey there, fellow travel enthusiast! Ready to embark on a journey that'll take your wanderlust to new heights? Well, buckle up because we're about to dive headfirst into the exciting world of travel planning and budgeting – tailor-made just for busy entrepreneurs like you!

In our trusty guide, "The Ultimate Guide on How To Plan and Budget for Travel," we've packed it to the brim with practical tips, savvy strategies, and insider insights to help you jet-set without burning a hole in your pocket. Yep, you heard that right – we're all about ensuring you have a blast on your adventures without breaking the bank.

So, what's in store for you? Well, consider this your one-stop shop for all things travel planning. From picking the perfect destination to setting your budget and beyond, we've got your back every step of the way.

In Chapter 2, we're kicking things off by guiding you through the thrilling process of choosing your dream destination and mapping out your travel budget. Say goodbye to decision fatigue as we help you narrow down your options based on interests, budget constraints, and those pesky travel restrictions.

Next up, in Chapter 3, we're hitting the road – or the skies – to explore a plethora of affordable transportation options. From flights to trains, buses, and rental cars, we've got the lowdown on how to score the best deals and save big on getting from point A to point B.

Now, let's talk digs! Accommodation can often be a budget-buster, but fear not – in Chapter 4, we're here to help you sniff out cozy stays that won't drain your bank account. Whether you're into hotels, hostels, vacation rentals, or even camping, we've got tips to ensure you sleep easy without breaking the bank.

But wait, there's more! Chapter 5 is all about crafting the ultimate itinerary packed with unforgettable experiences. From must-see attractions to off-the-beaten-path gems, we'll show you how to plan your daily adventures like a pro, all while keeping your budget in check.

Now, let's talk about everyone's favorite topic – food! Chapter 6 is serving up some tasty tips on budgeting for meals and dining out. From sampling local delicacies at street markets to packing picnic supplies for scenic lunches, we've got your taste buds covered without blowing your budget.

But what about those unexpected bumps in the road? Fear not – in Chapter 7, we're highlighting the importance of setting aside emergency funds and crafting contingency plans. From travel insurance to backup plans for unforeseen circumstances, we'll ensure you're prepared for anything life throws your way.

And because managing your finances on the fly doesn't have to be a headache, Chapter 8 is all about staying financially savvy while traveling. From handy budgeting tools to tips on tracking expenses and managing currency exchange rates, we've got your back every step of the way.

Now, let's talk about stretching those travel dollars! Chapter 9 is your ticket to unlocking a treasure trove of money-saving strategies. From travel rewards programs to snagging sweet discounts and freebies, we'll show you how to make your budget go the extra mile.

Last but not least, in Chapter 10, it's time to reflect on your travel adventures and fine-tune your budgeting strategies for future trips. We'll help you evaluate your expenses, reflect on your highlights, and adjust your budgeting game plan based on your experiences and feedback.

But hey, we're not just about doling out advice – we're all about sharing inspiring stories from fellow entrepreneurs who've nailed the art of planning and budgeting for their travels. So, are you ready to dive in and discover the magic of travel planning and budgeting? Let's make some memories, stay within budget, and explore the world like never before!

Chapter 1: Let's Talk Travel Planning and Budgeting

Hey there, fellow wanderers! Ready to embark on some epic adventures? Whether you're dreaming of sipping cocktails on a tropical beach or exploring ancient ruins in far-off lands, one thing's for sure: proper planning and budgeting are your ticket to a stress-free and unforgettable trip. So grab your passport and let's dive into the wonderful world of travel planning and budgeting!

Understanding the Importance of Effective Travel Planning and Budgeting

Let's face it: winging it might work for some things, but when it comes to travel, a little prep goes a long way. Here's why:

- **Stay organized:** Ever shown up at a hotel only to realize you booked the wrong dates? Yeah, not fun. Planning ahead keeps things smooth sailing from start to finish.
- **Maximize your experiences:** With a solid plan in place, you can hit all the hot spots and must-see sights without wasting a single minute.
- **Avoid overspending:** Budgeting isn't

just about pinching pennies—it's about making your money work for you. Know where every dollar is going so you can splurge where it counts.
- **Minimize financial stress:** Nothing kills the vibe faster than worrying about money. Stick to your budget and you'll be living your best life, stress-free.

Overview of Different Types of Travel Experiences

Not all who wander are lost, but knowing what kind of wanderer you are sure helps. Let's break it down:

- **Solo travel:** Ready to march to the beat of your own drum? Solo travel is all about freedom and self-discovery. Just don't forget to pack some extra courage for those moments of solitude.
- **Family vacations:** From screaming toddlers to moody teens, family vacations are a rollercoaster of chaos and joy. Embrace the chaos, plan some kid-friendly activities, and you'll make memories that'll last a lifetime.
- **Group trips:** Who says you have to go it alone? Grab your squad and hit the road together. Just be prepared for some epic adventures, a few squabbles, and memories that'll bond you for life.

Setting Goals and Objectives for Your Travel Adventures

Alright, time to get serious. What do you want to get out of this trip? Here are some questions to get those gears turning:

- What's your ultimate goal for this trip? Adventure? Relaxation? Cultural immersion?
- Any must-see sights or bucket list experiences you're itching to check off?
- What's your vibe? Are you craving bustling city streets or serene natural landscapes?
- Any cultural or educational experiences you're keen to dive into?
- And of course, what's your budget and timeframe looking like?

Once you've got your goals and objectives nailed down, you'll be ready to start planning your dream trip. But hold onto your boarding pass because in the next chapter, we're diving into the juicy stuff: choosing your destination and crafting that perfect travel budget. Ready, set, jet-set!

Chapter 2: Picking Your Dream Spot and Wallet-Friendly Plans

Alright, fellow travelers, let's get down to business! Choosing where to go and how much dough to dish out are the first big steps in planning your adventure. So, in this chapter, we're going to break down the art of researching destinations, estimating travel costs, and setting a budget that won't leave you singing the budget blues.

Exploring Potential Travel Destinations

Alright, buckle up—we're diving into the fun stuff: picking your dream destination! Start by brainstorming. Think about all the places you've ever dreamed of visiting or heard whispers about. Are you itching for cultural immersion, craving scenic vistas, or ready to dive into history? Jot down your top picks, then narrow it down based on your interests, budget, and any pesky travel restrictions. Love nature? Maybe a national park or beach destination is calling your name. History buff? Look into cities brimming with historical sites and museums. Once you've got a shortlist, it's time to dig deeper. Research local customs, safety tips, and the best times to visit. And don't forget to peek at the cost of living—your wallet will thank you later.

Estimating Travel Costs

Now, let's talk dollars and cents. Before you commit to a destination, you've gotta know what you're getting into financially. Start by breaking down your expenses. Think transportation, accommodation, food, activities, and all those little extras. First up, transportation. Compare prices for flights, trains, buses, or rental cars. Keep an eye out for seasonal price hikes and consider the distance between home and your destination. Next, scope out accommodation options. From swanky hotels to cozy hostels, there's something for every budget. And don't forget to factor in food costs. Are you a foodie who loves dining out, or are you packing sandwiches for the road? Know thyself, and budget accordingly. Lastly, leave room for activities, shopping, and any other splurges you're dreaming of.

Crafting a Realistic Travel Budget

Now that you've got a handle on the costs, it's time to crunch some numbers. Be real with yourself about what you can afford. A travel budget should be like a good yoga class—flexible and able to bend with the flow. Leave wiggle room for unexpected expenses and spontaneous adventures. Prioritize your spending. What's most important to you? Whether it's cozy digs or gourmet meals, allocate your funds wisely. Remember, it's all about finding that sweet spot between living your best life and keeping your bank account happy.

Wrapping Up

Alright, adventurers, you're armed with the knowledge to pick your dream spot and set a budget that won't break the bank. But hold onto your hats because the next chapter is all about snagging wallet-friendly transportation options. So, pack your bags and get ready for the journey of a lifetime!

Chapter 3: Finding Budget-Friendly Transportation

Hey there, savvy traveler! Ready to dive into the world of budget-friendly transportation options? In this chapter, we're going to be your virtual tour guides, showing you the ropes on how to get from point A to point B without blowing your budget. Let's roll!

Exploring Your Transportation Options

First things first – let's talk about the different modes of transportation at your disposal. From zipping through the skies to chugging along scenic railways, there's a plethora of options to choose from:

Flights: Ah, the classic choice for jet setters! Flying can be speedy and convenient, especially for long-haul journeys. But don't hit that "book now" button just yet – shop around for deals and consider nabbing a round-trip ticket for extra savings.

Trains: All aboard the budget-friendly express! Trains offer a laid-back way to travel, perfect for soaking in breathtaking views and mingling with fellow wanderers. Keep an eye out for discounted fares and consider snagging a rail pass if you're planning to hop between destinations.

Buses: For the frugal traveler, buses are a wallet-friendly dream. Whether you're embarking on a short jaunt or exploring a specific region, buses offer comfy rides at pocket-friendly prices. Pro tip: Opt for overnight buses to save on accommodation costs – it's a win-win!

Rental Cars: Need a set of wheels for your grand adventure? Renting a car can be a game-changer, giving you the freedom to explore off-the-beaten-path destinations. Just remember to compare prices, factor in insurance coverage, and keep an eye out for hidden fees.

Walking or Cycling: Sometimes, the best way to experience a destination is on foot or by bike. Lace up your sneakers or hop on a bicycle and hit the streets – you'll not only save on transportation costs but also get a taste of local life along the way.

Comparing Prices Like a Pro

Now that you've got your transportation options laid out, it's time to snag the best deals in town. Here's how to score big on savings:

Comparison Websites: Say hello to your new best friends – comparison websites! Platforms like Skyscanner and Kayak are treasure troves of deals, helping you compare prices across airlines, trains, and buses. Plus, they dish out handy tips on the cheapest travel times and alternate routes – jackpot!

Flexibility Is Key: Want to unlock secret savings? Be flexible with your travel dates and times. Flying midweek or during off-peak seasons can lead to major discounts, while overnight journeys can score you extra savings on accommodation costs. Keep an open mind, and you'll reap the rewards!

Watch Out for Sneaky Fees: Ah, the dreaded extra fees – they're the bane of every budget traveler's existence. When comparing prices, be sure to factor in pesky add-ons like baggage fees and seat selection charges. A little vigilance now can save you big bucks later!

Loyalty Pays Off: If you're a frequent flyer or train hopper, consider joining loyalty programs or credit card reward schemes. Accumulating points and miles can unlock sweet discounts and even free travel down the line – talk about a win-win!

Crafting Your Perfect Itinerary

Now that you've got your transportation sorted, it's time to map out your journey like a pro. Here are some tips to help you make the most of your travel itinerary:

Location, Location, Location: When choosing accommodations, opt for a central spot that's a stone's throw away from public transportation hubs or must-see attractions. This way, you'll spend less time and money on getting around – win!

Group Activities by Location: Want to streamline your sightseeing? Group your daily activities by location to minimize travel time and costs. By clustering attractions together, you'll make the most of your precious time on the ground.

Factor in Buffer Time: Murphy's Law – anything that can go wrong, will go wrong. When crafting your itinerary, leave some wiggle room for unexpected delays or transportation hiccups. Trust us – a little buffer time goes a long way in keeping your stress levels in check.

Embrace Overnight Travel: Got a long journey ahead? Consider hopping on an overnight train or bus. Not only will you save on accommodation costs, but you'll also wake up in a brand-new destination, ready to hit the ground running. Talk about making the most of your time!

And there you have it – a crash course in finding budget-friendly transportation options for your next adventure. By exploring different modes of transportation, comparing prices like a pro, and crafting a savvy itinerary, you'll be well on your way to exploring the world without breaking the bank. So, strap in and get ready for the ride of a lifetime – adventure awaits!

Chapter 4: Let's Talk Accommodations: Finding Your Home Away from Home

Alright, fellow travelers, let's talk about where you're gonna rest your weary head after a day of exploring. Because let's face it, finding the perfect accommodation can make or break your travel experience. But fear not! We're here to guide you through the maze of options and help you find the perfect place that won't break the bank.

Exploring Accommodation Options

From swanky hotels to cozy cottages, the world of accommodations is your oyster. Here's a rundown of your options:

1. **Hotels:** Whether you're a budget traveler or a luxury seeker, hotels have got you covered. Just be sure to check out the location, ratings, and reviews before you book.
2. **Hostels:** If you're flying solo or on a tight budget, hostels are your new best friend. With shared dorms and a social vibe, they're perfect for making new friends and saving some cash.
3. **Vacation rentals:** Want to live like a local? Vacation rentals like apartments

or houses offer space, privacy, and a homey feel. Plus, you can save some dough by cooking your own meals.
4. **Camping sites:** Calling all nature lovers! Camping is not only budget-friendly but also a great way to get up close and personal with Mother Nature. Just make sure you're prepared for some outdoor adventure.

Setting Criteria for Choosing Accommodations

So, what exactly should you be looking for in your dream accommodation? Here are a few things to consider:

1. **Location:** Do you want to be in the heart of the action or somewhere a bit more tranquil? Consider accessibility to attractions and amenities when choosing your location.
2. **Amenities:** Make a list of must-have amenities like Wi-Fi, breakfast, or a gym. Then, prioritize them based on what's important to you and your budget.
3. **Price:** Ah, the big one. Set a budget and stick to it! Prices can vary depending on location and season, so keep an eye out for deals and be flexible with your travel dates.

4. **Reviews:** Don't just take our word for it—listen to the people! Check out online reviews to get the lowdown on accommodations from past guests.

Using Online Booking Platforms and Apps

Ready to dive into the world of online booking? Here's how to make the most of it:

1. **Comparison websites:** Sites like Booking.com, Expedia, and Airbnb are your besties when it comes to comparing prices and reviews. Use them to your advantage!
2. **Filter options:** Narrow down your search by filtering based on price, location, and amenities. Trust us, it'll save you a ton of time scrolling through endless options.
3. **Special deals and discounts:** Keep your eyes peeled for those sweet deals and discounts. You never know when you'll snag a bargain!
4. **Secure reservations:** Once you've found the perfect spot, lock it in! Just be sure to read the fine print on cancellations and refunds.

By exploring your options, setting your criteria,

and mastering the art of online booking, you'll be well on your way to finding accommodations that fit your budget and your travel style. So go ahead, book that dream stay, and get ready for the adventure of a lifetime!

Chapter 5: Let's Plan Your Daily Adventures and Epic Experiences

Alright, fellow adventurers, it's time to lace up those boots and dive into the nitty-gritty of planning your daily escapades! Trust me, when it comes to travel, mapping out your activities is just as important as budgeting. So, in this chapter, we're going to walk you through the art of researching, prioritizing, and budgeting for all those unforgettable moments waiting for you at your destination.

Scouring and Sorting Activities, Attractions, and Experiences

Alright, let's start this journey off right—with some good old-fashioned research. Before you set foot on that plane or hop in the car, take a deep dive into all the amazing activities and attractions your destination has to offer. Make a list of everything that catches your eye, from iconic landmarks to hidden gems off the beaten path. Think about what gets your heart racing and your curiosity piqued. Are you itching to explore ancient ruins, taste exotic street food, or zip-line through the jungle? Whatever floats your boat, jot it down. Then, narrow it down based on what truly speaks to your soul. Consider your time, budget, and logistical constraints. After all, you don't want to rush through a museum or miss out on a once-in-a-lifetime experience because you're double-booked.

Budgeting for Adventures, Tours, and More

Now, let's talk cash flow. Once you've got your list of dream activities, it's time to crunch some numbers. Research the costs of entrance fees, guided tours, excursions, and any other adventures that make your heart skip a beat. And don't forget to factor in those sneaky additional expenses, like transportation or gear rental. Allocate a chunk of your travel budget to cover these costs. But remember, not all adventures are created equal. Some may be splurge-worthy, while others are best enjoyed on a shoestring budget. So, strike a balance. Maybe splurge on that hot air balloon ride over the countryside, but balance it out with a leisurely stroll through a local market. And if you're traveling with pals, hash out your budget and activity wish list together. Collaboration is key to crafting an unforgettable trip that everyone will love.

Crafting a Flexible Game Plan

Now, here's the kicker: flexibility. Sure, having a plan is great, but being able to roll with the punches? That's where the real magic happens. Give yourself some breathing room in your itinerary. Schedule in downtime for rest, relaxation, and unexpected detours. Trust me, some of the best adventures happen when you least expect them. Be open to recommendations from locals or fellow travelers you meet along the way. Sometimes the most memorable experiences come from stepping off the beaten path and diving headfirst into the unknown. And hey, don't forget to sprinkle in some free or low-cost activities too. Many destinations offer parks, markets, and walking tours that pack a punch without draining your wallet. By blending must-see attractions with budget-friendly adventures, you'll create a travel experience that's as rich in memories as it is in culture.

Wrapping Up

Alright, fellow wanderers, you're armed with the tools to plan your daily escapades like a pro. But hold onto your hats because the next chapter is all about snagging those wallet-friendly transportation options. So, get ready to hit the road and make some unforgettable memories along the way!

Chapter 6: Navigating Food Costs on Your Travels

Hey there, hungry traveler! Let's talk about one of the most mouthwatering parts of your journey – the food! From savoring local delicacies to grabbing a quick bite on the go, dining experiences can make or break your travel budget. But fear not, because in this chapter, we're serving up some tasty tips on how to estimate food costs and dine like a champ without burning a hole in your wallet.

Planning Your Dining Budget

First things first – let's dish out some wisdom on budgeting for meals and dining out. Here's how to whip up a budget that satisfies both your taste buds and your wallet:

1. **Scout Out Local Food Prices:** Before you embark on your adventure, do a little digging on the average cost of meals at your destination. This savvy move gives you a ballpark figure to work with and helps you avoid any pricey surprises down the road.
2. **Know Thy Eating Habits:** Are you a culinary connoisseur who lives for Michelin-starred meals, or are you more of a street food aficionado? Tailor your

budget to match your dining preferences and decide how often you'll be eating out versus cooking in.
3. **Consider Your Dietary Needs:** Got any dietary restrictions or preferences? Whether you're gluten-free, vegan, or just a picky eater, it's essential to factor in any special dietary requirements that might affect your food budget. Trust us – a little planning goes a long way!

Exploring Affordable Dining Options

Now that we've got your budget sorted, let's dive into the delicious world of affordable dining options. Here are some mouthwatering suggestions to satisfy your cravings without breaking the bank:

1. **Hit Up Local Food Markets:** Craving an authentic taste of local flavor? Head to bustling food markets brimming with fresh produce, tantalizing treats, and wallet-friendly eats. Grab some goodies to cook up a storm or enjoy a picnic in the park – it's a win-win!
2. **Embrace Street Food:** Ready to tantalize your taste buds with street-side delights? Seek out vibrant street food scenes and indulge in an array of tasty treats. Not only is street food delicious, but it's also easy on the wallet – just

make sure to pick vendors with stellar hygiene practices!
3. **Seek Out Hidden Gems:** Tired of tourist traps and overpriced eateries? Venture off the beaten path and discover local haunts favored by savvy locals. From hole-in-the-wall joints to mom-and-pop diners, these hidden gems offer authentic flavors at unbeatable prices.

Packing Snacks for the Road

Last but not least, let's talk snacks! Packing your own munchies is not only a money-savvy move but also a lifesaver on long travel days. Here are some snack-tastic ideas to keep your hunger at bay:

1. **Stock Up on Non-Perishables:** Load up on travel-friendly snacks like granola bars, trail mix, or dried fruit to keep hunger pangs at bay during transit. These portable treats are perfect for fueling your adventures without breaking the bank.
2. **Pack Picnic Essentials:** Want to dine al fresco while soaking in scenic views? Pack a small cooler, reusable water bottle, and some handy utensils for impromptu picnics. Grab fresh goodies from local markets and enjoy a

budget-friendly feast in the great outdoors!

Remember, while it's essential to stick to your budget, don't forget to savor the flavors of your destination. Sampling local cuisines and exploring culinary delights is all part of the travel experience. So go ahead, indulge your taste buds, and make delicious memories along the way! Next up, in Chapter 7, we'll chat about the importance of setting aside emergency funds and crafting contingency plans for your travels. Bon appétit!

Chapter 7: Be Ready for Anything: Emergency Funds and Backup Plans

Alright, fellow adventurers, let's talk about the unexpected twists and turns that can happen when you're out exploring the world. No matter how meticulously you plan, life has a funny way of throwing curveballs your way. That's why it's absolutely crucial to have a safety net in place—a little something we like to call emergency funds and contingency plans.

Why Emergency Funds Matter

Picture this: You're halfway across the globe, soaking in the sights and sounds of a bustling city when suddenly, disaster strikes. Maybe it's a sudden illness, a canceled flight, or—gasp!—lost luggage. Having emergency funds tucked away can be a total game-changer. Think of it as your financial lifeline, ready to rescue you from whatever curveballs travel throws your way.

How to Set Aside Emergency Funds

So, how much should you stash away for a rainy day? While there's no one-size-fits-all answer, setting aside around 10% of your total travel budget is a good rule of thumb. Of course, the exact amount will depend on your personal circumstances and comfort level. The key is to have enough cushion to cover unexpected expenses without breaking the bank.

But Wait, There's More: Travel Insurance

Emergency funds are just the first line of defense. For added peace of mind, consider investing in travel insurance. Think of it as your ultimate safety net, protecting you from everything from flight cancellations to medical emergencies. Just be sure to read the fine print and choose a policy that fits your needs and travel plans like a glove.

Crafting Your Contingency Plan

Alright, now onto the nitty-gritty: crafting your contingency plan. It might not be the most exciting part of trip planning, but trust us, it's worth it. Here's what you need to consider:

1. **Backup Accommodation:** Keep a list of alternative accommodation options handy in case your original plans fall through. You never know when a hotel might overbook or a rental might turn out to be less than stellar.
2. **Transportation Plan B:** When it comes

to travel, expect the unexpected. Have a backup plan for getting around, whether it's hopping on public transport, renting a car, or hitching a ride with a friendly local.
3. **Flexibility is Key:** Embrace the chaos and roll with the punches. A loosely structured itinerary gives you the freedom to adapt to whatever curveballs come your way.
4. **Stay Connected:** Make sure you've got reliable communication options, whether it's a local SIM card or a trusty Wi-Fi connection. Being able to reach out for help or updates can be a total game-changer in a pinch.

Final Thoughts

Remember, fellow travelers, being prepared is the name of the game. Setting aside emergency funds, investing in travel insurance, and crafting a solid contingency plan might not be the most glamorous part of trip planning, but trust us, it's worth it. So go ahead, embrace the adventure, and rest easy knowing you've got a safety net to catch you if things don't go as planned. Safe travels!

Chapter 8: Money Matters: Mastering Your Finances on the Fly

Alright, fellow jet-setters, let's talk dough. Managing your finances and keeping tabs on expenses while you're out gallivanting around the globe? It's kind of a big deal. So, in this chapter, we're diving into the world of savvy strategies and handy tools that'll keep your budget in check while you're on the move.

Harnessing the Power of Budgeting Tools and Apps

First things first: tracking those expenses. Lucky for us, we live in the age of technology, where there's an app for just about everything—including managing your moolah. Budgeting tools like Mint, You Need a Budget (YNAB), and PocketGuard are your new best friends. They let you record and categorize your expenses on the fly, giving you a bird's-eye view of where your cash is flowing. Plus, they sync up with your bank accounts and credit cards, so you can stay on top of your spending in real-time. And hey, if you're old school, a good ol' spreadsheet works wonders too. Just whip one up with different expense categories, like accommodation, transportation, meals, and activities, and update it as you go.

Keeping an Eye on Exchange Rates and Fees

Now, let's talk foreign currency. When you're trotting the globe, those exchange rates can make or break your budget. So, stay in the know. Keep tabs on exchange rates using handy online platforms and mobile apps that give you real-time updates. And when it comes to swapping your cash, stick to reputable spots like banks or authorized currency exchange offices to avoid getting gouged with fees. Oh, and don't forget about those sneaky transaction fees that come with using your credit or debit cards abroad. Some cards offer perks like no foreign transaction fees, so it's worth checking out your options before you jet off. And for good measure, give your bank a heads-up about your travel plans to avoid any hiccups with your cards.

Setting Limits and Prioritizing Spending

Alright, let's talk strategy. To keep your spending in check, start by setting some limits. Figure out a daily or weekly budget that jibes with your overall travel budget, factoring in essentials like accommodation, transport, and grub. Once you've got your budget nailed down, it's time to prioritize. What experiences are non-negotiables for you? Maybe you're all about diving with sharks or slurping down street food in Bangkok. Whatever floats your boat, allocate more funds to the stuff that lights your fire. And hey, be prepared to make some trade-offs. Maybe skip that fancy dinner and opt for a picnic in the park instead. Your wallet will thank you later.

Wrapping Up

Alright, globetrotters, you're officially armed with the knowledge to master your finances while you're out chasing adventures. But hey, stick around because in the next chapter, we're dishing out some killer tips to help you stretch your travel budget even further. So, buckle up and get ready to make some epic memories without breaking the bank!

Chapter 9: Unveiling Travel Budget Hacks

Hey savvy traveler, ready to unlock the secrets of stretching your travel budget? In this chapter, we're diving deep into the realm of money-saving strategies that'll have you jet-setting without emptying your pockets. Let's get started!

1. **Mastering Travel Rewards Programs:** Picture this – earning points or miles every time you swipe your card, which you can later redeem for free flights and hotel stays. That's the magic of travel rewards programs! Whether it's airlines, hotels, or credit card companies, there's a plethora of options out there. Do your homework, find one that suits your spending habits, and watch those rewards rack up.
2. **Embracing Credit Card Perks:** Your trusty credit card might just be your ticket to a world of perks and benefits tailor-made for travelers. From travel insurance to airport lounge access, some cards roll out the red carpet for globetrotters. Take a moment to check out the perks your card offers – you might be pleasantly surprised!
3. **Pledging Allegiance to Loyalty Programs:** Ever stayed loyal to a hotel

chain or airline and reaped the rewards? Loyalty programs are a traveler's best friend, showering you with discounts, upgrades, and exclusive perks. Stick with your favorites, accumulate those points, and watch your savings soar.
4. **Scouting for Discounts and Offers:** Before you hit that "book now" button, pause for a moment and scour the web for discounts, coupons, and special deals. Many destinations roll out the red carpet for budget-conscious travelers with tourist passes and city cards that unlock a treasure trove of savings. It pays to do your research!

Capitalizing on Deals and Offers

Now that you've got the lowdown on money-saving strategies let's dive into some pro tips for making the most of those discounts and special offers:

1. **Arm Yourself with Knowledge:** Knowledge is power, especially when it comes to scoring sweet deals. Take the time to compare prices across different platforms and sniff out those hidden gems. Whether it's accommodations, flights, or activities, a little comparison goes a long way.
2. **Stay in the Loop:** Want the inside

scoop on exclusive deals and offers? Sign up for newsletters from your favorite travel websites, airlines, and hotels. You'll be the first to know about flash sales, last-minute deals, and insider tips – talk about VIP treatment!
3. **Flexibility Is Key:** Want to score big on savings? Stay flexible with your travel dates and destinations. Off-peak seasons and weekdays are your best friends when it comes to snagging discounted fares and accommodations. Keep an open mind, and you might just stumble upon your next budget-friendly adventure.
4. **Crack the Coupon Code:** Don't hit that checkout button without a quick search for coupons and promo codes. Websites like Groupon and RetailMeNot are treasure troves of discounts on activities, attractions, and dining options. A few clicks could mean big savings – it's a win-win!

Uncovering Free and Low-Cost Entertainment

Who says the best things in life aren't free? When it comes to entertainment and experiences, there's a whole world of budget-friendly options waiting to be explored:

1. **Nature's Playground:** Step into the great outdoors and immerse yourself in nature's beauty. From scenic hikes to sunset beach strolls, Mother Nature provides the ultimate backdrop for free entertainment and relaxation.
2. **Market Magic:** Dive into the heart of the local culture by exploring bustling food markets, craft fairs, and flea markets. Sample mouthwatering treats, pick up unique souvenirs, and soak in the vibrant atmosphere – all without spending a dime.
3. **Festivals and Fun:** Keep your eyes peeled for local festivals and events happening during your stay. From music and dance to food and folklore, these celebrations offer a glimpse into the soul of a destination – and the best part? They're often free!
4. **Museum Mania:** Culture vultures, rejoice! Many museums and cultural institutions offer free admission on select days or times. It's your chance to dive into history, art, and culture without reaching for your wallet.
5. **Park Life:** Take a breather and enjoy some downtime in a local park or garden. Pack a picnic, people-watch, or simply bask in the beauty of your surroundings – it's the perfect way to unwind without spending a penny.

By mastering money-saving strategies, capitalizing on deals and offers, and uncovering free or low-cost entertainment options, you're well on your way to becoming a budget-savvy traveler extraordinaire. Remember, it's not just about saving money – it's about crafting unforgettable experiences and connecting with the world around you. So go ahead, embrace adventure, and make every penny count!

Chapter 10: Learning from Your Adventure: Reflecting on Your Travel Experience and Budgeting Smarts

Alright, fellow wanderers, let's take a moment to reflect on the journey we've just embarked upon. Whether you've traversed distant lands or explored hidden gems in your own backyard, every adventure is a chance to learn, grow, and, of course, tweak those budgeting strategies for future escapades. So, grab a cup of tea, find a cozy spot, and let's dive into the art of reflection and budget adjustment.

Taking Stock of Your Travel Budget

As you bid adieu to your latest adventure, it's time to crunch some numbers and see how your budget held up. Take a look at your initial budget estimates and compare them to your actual expenses. Did you stay on track, or did you veer off course somewhere along the way? Maybe you splurged on a once-in-a-lifetime experience or snagged a sweet deal on accommodations. Whatever the case, jot down any surprises, both pleasant and not-so-pleasant, that cropped up during your journey.

Now, let's get down to the nitty-gritty. Break down your expenses into categories like accommodations, transportation, dining, activities, and souvenirs. This little exercise will help you pinpoint where your money went and where you might have room to tighten the purse strings next time around. Maybe you found yourself indulging in gourmet meals but skimping on transportation costs. Understanding these spending patterns is key to honing your budgeting skills for future adventures.

Reflecting on Your Travel Moments

Ah, now for the fun part—reflecting on the moments that made your heart sing and your soul soar. Think back to those awe-inspiring sunsets, those chance encounters with locals, and those belly laughs shared with newfound friends. These are the memories that will stay with you long after the trip is over.

But it's not just about reliving the highlights; it's about learning from the journey itself. Did you stumble upon any genius travel hacks or budgeting tricks that saved the day? Maybe you discovered the joys of street food or mastered the art of haggling at local markets. Take note of these nuggets of wisdom—they'll come in handy on future adventures.

Adjusting Your Budgeting Game Plan

Armed with newfound insights and a fresh perspective, it's time to fine-tune your budgeting strategies for the next adventure on the horizon. Here's the game plan:

1. **Update Your Budget:** Take everything you've learned from your reflections and use it to craft a shiny new budget for your next escapade. Maybe you'll allocate more funds for those unforgettable experiences and a little less for those everyday expenses.
2. **Shift Your Priorities:** If you found yourself overspending in certain areas, consider reallocating funds to areas that bring you the most joy. Maybe you'll trade fancy dinners for museum visits or splurge on accommodations that offer a touch of luxury.
3. **Set New Savings Goals:** Based on your budget evaluation, set realistic savings goals for your next adventure. If you overspent last time, no worries—just adjust your targets and get back on track.
4. **Embrace New Adventures:** Reflecting on your travel experiences might inspire you to try something new on your next trip. Whether it's backpacking through rugged landscapes or immersing

yourself in local culture, let your reflections guide your future adventures.
5. **Seek Wisdom from Fellow Travelers:** Connect with fellow adventurers to swap stories, share tips, and gather insights for your next journey. Online forums and travel communities are treasure troves of knowledge just waiting to be discovered.

Remember, fellow explorers, reflection is the compass that guides us on our journey. By taking the time to evaluate our travel experiences and adjust our budgeting strategies accordingly, we can ensure that every adventure is not just memorable but also financially savvy. So here's to many more adventures, filled with priceless moments and budgeting smarts! Cheers!